DONAL NE

Who do you say that I am?

and other Gospel questions

VERITAS

First published 2001 by
Veritas Publications
7/8 Lower Abbey Street
Dublin 1
Ireland

Email publications@veritas.ie
Website www.veritas.ie

ISBN 1 85390 514 3

Cover design by Bill Bolger
Printed in the Republic of Ireland by Betaprint Ltd, Dublin

Contents

WHO DOES HE SAY THAT WE ARE?

Introduction

A way of introducing a book is to say what it has done for the author. In writing these reflections I discovered that Jesus was a man of many questions. I like that, because I have found more help in my life from people who encouraged me to ask the right questions rather than who tried to give me many answers. Life is mostly about living the questions, of discovering God within our questions and yearnings, of growing into meaning and finding directions towards answers.

The questions of Jesus are probing and they are gentle. They don't harass; they are asked and then we are left to explore their meaning. Some of his questions, as in the first part of the book – *Who do you say that I am?* – direct us towards who Jesus is for us; in the second part – *Who does he say that we are?* – the questions are more about our following of him.

Each of his questions is followed, not by an answer, but the direction towards an answer. As if he says, 'If you want to answer the question, "What do you want?", you'll find the answer somewhere along the path, "Come and See".' Or when you don't understand what Jesus is doing, like the washing of the feet, you find the direction to an answer in just doing what he does, for our Christian life is best understood in our efforts to live it. Those who try to love to the end know what God is like.

We find a gentleness and humanity in Jesus that is exciting and exhilarating. We find that the heart of God is a place of humanity, and of safety on the journey of life. With Jesus we find a way of being with people that respects all the big human questions.

These reflections will touch off the tones and moods of the question in the reader. They are best read slowly, not all at once. They may be read as a beginning to pray the gospel passage of which they are part. They do not, obviously, exhaust the questions of Jesus nor do they attempt to cover all the Christian life. They can be used in prayer groups, in liturgy, personal prayer or reflection, and hopefully will introduce the reader to the questioning heart of Jesus.

Donal Neary SJ

WHO DO
YOU SAY THAT I AM?

Hearing them and asking them questions
(Luke 2:46)

The child and the man –
the way Jesus was in the temple,
the child listening and asking questions,
points the way to his future attitude,
and his relationships to the learned and the simple.

A listener to people's experience and questions:
to where people came from and where they were at.
Valuing what his listeners themselves
believed and valued;
alive to their struggles and pain,
their hopes, fears, griefs, anxieties;
present with us in those spaces where
we laugh and cry, dance and grieve,
love and hate, fear and hope,
present to us in the hungers of our heart.

He communicates that what is important to us
is important to God.

We think God might not be concerned
with the ordinary concerns of human life,
like worries about the children,
job worries and career choices,
sexuality with its conflicts,
ups and downs of moods,
the special intentions we pray for.
All are part of our relationship with God.

Jesus could hear experience as well as our words.
In his life we notice his sympathy and compassion
        with people,
at a well, in a crowd, on a cross beside him,
and a sensitivity to his friends' struggles
with faith and hope after his resurrection.

Through the questions of Jesus in the gospel,
we find a direction towards an answer.

Questions don't go away,
they become the table of contents
to a book of meaning and wholeness.

If we live the questions,
we will be led into answers
by the God of the questions.

Is it not relevant that the first words of Jesus
in the gospels of Luke and of John
are questions that flow through all of life:

'Why were you looking for me?'
'What do you want?'
With those questions we can live
happily, fully, yet never satisfied;
for God and self are like a sea always deeper,
a mountain beckoning higher step by step,
and a love more deeply exhilarating.

Why were you looking for me? Did you not know that I was about my Father's business?

(Luke 2:49)

A strange question to his mother and Joseph –
is it not reasonable that they would look for Jesus,
lost or astray on a journey and he only twelve?

From the outset Jesus is stating
the direction and meaning of his life;
like rivers flow to the sea,
like lighthouses guide in the dark,
like reservoirs store water,
his eye is fixed – and his heart too –
on what is important to his Father.

With this question we discover
what we might make sacrifices for –
of time, money, comfort, desires.
Or what we think of in stray moments
like last thing at night or first in the morning.
And what we get really excited or sad about.
These are the things we are busy about.

To find something big enough to be busy about
is a gift and a meaning in life;
the actions of Jesus and his concerns
are the most energising motivations
of all love, desire, hope and vision.

And the concerns of Jesus are the concerns of God.

They did not understand what he meant

(Luke 2:50)

People would often not understand
that Jesus' life came from a space where God lived:
the Word through whom all things were made,
lives in the presence of God and people,
for he is God-made-flesh, Emmanuel.

Do we not try to categorise Jesus?
A political leader, a revolutionary,
a certain personality type,
try to understand him with names
like Mercy, Heart, Blood?

No name defines him;
all that he says of himself and all that we call him
help us appreciate and delve into the mystery
of who he is for us, and who he is with God.

We cannot understand Jesus
unless we know his deep love for his Father:
his passions for justice and reconciliation
are appreciated only in knowing that
the desires and motivations of his life
were centred on his Father,
for he lived in God.
His willingness to go to the end of human love
was his way of showing us divine love.

Love for humanity, for Jesus as for ourselves,
was the way to show his love for God.

Who do you say that I am?

(Matthew 16:15)

What we say of God is a statement about ourselves,
and points to a direction in life.
Our answer will answer big questions,
like what life is for,
what real love and justice is,
what happens after death,
and what God means.
Questions that echo fully at times of depth in life.

Whatever we think of Jesus
says something about our view of ourselves.

When we name Jesus,
we are saying something important about ourselves,
and what we believe is central to our lives.

Saying that Jesus is the Son of God
means we believe in eternity,
that we believe that God is loving.
It means also that we know we are God's children,
and that all love is a share in the life of eternity.
If we know who Jesus is,
then we know the fullness of life
and the love of the One
who has made his home in us.

And Jesus himself tells us something –
that he would die, suffer and be raised.
That's the answer about all of us –
we are destined for death and resurrection.
Whatever we say of Jesus the Christ,
we say of ourselves.

You are a happy man; because it was not flesh and blood that revealed this to you, but my Father in heaven (Matthew 16:17)

We can give all sorts of answers to this question,
'Who do people, who do you, say that I am?'
We can mouth answers others gave,
we can water down the real meaning of who he is,
as we can water down the real meaning of anyone
to suit ourselves.

The challenge is to go inside ourselves
to those places of
questioning, struggle and meaning,
and discover what we think of Jesus.

In these depths of ourselves
are the wellsprings of God's word,
which gives us the gift of faith;
a gift wrapped in the faith of others.

What others say of God and of Jesus,
sharing the depths of faith
in the depths of humanity,
can be a revelation of God.

Many hear, and some believe;
many believe, and some commit life to their belief.
Faith is more than what we hear and others hear;
it is a grace of God to each in our own way.

The answer is never solitary.
We discover what God says of Jesus
among people with whom we belong.

What do you want?

(John 1:38)

The first question of Jesus in the gospel,
to the disciples who were wondering
about following the Messiah.

We are men and women of many desires:
for success, happiness, peace,
for control of our lives and for security,
attaching ourselves to important people,
getting into casual relationships,
pretending to be what we're not.
And within all our desires,
we yearn and long to be loved.

It is a dangerous question,
because what we really want
can be masked by other desires,
and what we really want takes time to find:
to find acceptance and love,
to find a cause in life to give ourselves to,
to find joy and happiness,
even in illness, pain, depression, confusion.

Our deepest desire is to love and be loved.
We yearn for this like a river flows to the sea,
like a rainbow searches for all its colours,
like people in conflict long for peace.

When we find the consistent love of another
and the unconditional love of God
we have found life's greatest gifts.

Come and see

A good person will often bring out the best in us,
and a saint reminds us of how good we could be.

Jesus' answer to finding our desires
is simply to come and see him;
to watch where he lives,
how he heals and speaks,
to see what makes him happy
and how his life is single-minded.
To watch his kindness and his humour,
his real concern and love.

There is a quality of presence among some people:
among people in a hospice for the very ill,
or in a L'Arche community for the handicapped,
with their immediate sense of love and sincerity.
Or in a school for the poorest of the poor
with a taste for hope and life
within severe deprivation and poverty.

No lectures, no exhortation,
just being in the fragrant presence
of kindness, love,
and a passion for justice.

To find out where he lives is the search of life:
finding him within his creation,
within the people who follow him,
finding him who makes his home in each of us.

Can you drink the cup that I must drink, be baptised with the baptism with which I must be baptised? (Mark 10:38)

They had asked for places of honour –
two of Jesus' long-term disciples,
and he spoke about drinking the cup
of salvation, suffering and love,
and being baptised like him
in waters of service and justice.

The cup would be bitter wine,
the baptism would be total drowning;
like prison sentences for following ideals of justice,
like rejection by the family for obeying the gospel.

Like the consistent living of marriage vows
through thick and thin,
like consistent love of children in bad times,
like constant caring for the elderly in their
        weakness.

The cup would always be full
and the baptism would be daily renewed,
in the joy and pain
of living in love.

Love is lived in the shadow of pain
and struggles are never far away.
Like the joy of the tree
when a thorn bursts through,
like the huge joy at the birth of a child,
there is joy and fulfilment
on the pathways of love.

The Son of Man did not come to be served, but to serve

(Mark 10:45)

Humility, lowliness and service seen no longer
as a cul-de-sac to nowhere,
but as the highway of God,
the open way to freedom and joy –
and materialistic goals are turned upside down.

The expectation was that the leaders
would enjoy privileges and perks of honour,
and those with them would share the perks.
The way of Jesus reforms our view of privilege.

The privileged ones on the highway of God
are people seen as lowly by others:
shepherds, the first to hear of the birth of God,
women with shameful illnesses highlighted,
and sinners, the ones he shared his table with.

His command to his disciples was
that religion would care for the little ones,
would think it worthwhile to
look after the dying,
fight for the unborn,
and honour the poor.

True religion honours us for being ourselves,
created each day by the living word of God,
praised by God for who we are,
and for what we try to do in his service.

All are the delight of God.
And the one called King
is better known as Servant.

Is it against the law on the Sabbath to do good, or to do evil, to save life or destroy it? (Luke 6:9)

When human law is preferred to human aspirations,
the book highlighted over compassion,
in emphasis on the non-essentials,
what started as a sincere ritual
becomes frozen in the stony heart of religion.

People would be left ill on the sabbath,
because work was forbidden that day.
Fears would replace freedom
in the hearts and minds of good people.

True religion is summarised in many ways –
living a balance of worship, friendship and justice,
three streams of the river of God.

Our rituals are expressions of faith,
but if faith is cold or dead,
rituals become burdens, and true religion dies,
like fireworks that splutter before their time,
like a sentence that can't be completed,
like a CD stuck on one song.

Rituals and law created to bring life to the full
may bring hatred, division and deadness.
Questions of Jesus open us,
like getting to know someone really well,
open us to freeing truths,
for in his questions is the light of truth.

He looked around and said to the man, 'Stretch out your hand'

(Luke 6:10)

The time for the sermon was over,
words had said all that could be said,
minds were closed,
and all that would make sense
would be action.

The cure was the sermon,
the restored hand was the newness of religion.
and life would never be the same again,
for the man with the withered hand and for
        everyone.

True religion is witnessed, acted,
not just spoken, ritualised.

People rescuing children from abuse,
carers tending the elderly,
defenders of the sacredness of all life,
protectors of forests and rivers,
welcomers of refugees and foreigners,
all restoring life, caring for life.

When we care for life, we care for religion.

It's a two way process –
God stretches compassion and truth out to us,
and we reach to him in our need for enlightenment.
In the touch of the divine and the human,
is the birth of religion,
for religion is based on knowing
that God is near,
that humanity is one family,
and that life is the victor over death.

For who is the greater:
the one at table or the one who serves?

(Luke 22:27)

Who is the first around here?
Who has the power and the influence?
Questions that we ask directly or indirectly
in almost every group we belong to,
and the disciples of Jesus were no exception.

Displays of titles and dress in the church,
competitiveness in the family,
places of honour and mixing with the right people,
power in business and at work –
Jesus faced the question with the disciples.

They murmured among themselves often –
who was the one closest to the Lord,
who would be the leader, or mind the money.
Big questions when the mind is small,
or maybe the heart is angry or anxious.

His words opposed human competitiveness –
names and titles isolate us from each other,
and hide that we are all equal children of God.

The judgment of greatness and leadership,
of who is first and last
is made in the light of future death and resurrection;
he is remembered as the one who served at table,
who washed the feet, who favoured the poor
and who served to the end at the table of the cross.

Yet I am among you as one who serves

(Luke 22:27)

If we want to discover what's important to God,
we look at the way Jesus lived,
and enter into the heart of God
in the human heart of Jesus.

The way of service is the way of God,
it is the way of the cross and resurrection.

There are empty promises of happiness,
like wealth, casual relationships, comfort,
looking after self first.

The way of Jesus is the way of service –
being present with people and helping them
in times of worry and problems,
in the confusion of bringing up a family,
in living in the real human joy of love.

It's a way of service which tries
to make the world a more equal place for all,
and to enhance the human dignity of everyone.

We follow this service in our way of life
and know that the key to happiness and to God
is in placing our energies
for the betterment of people
for the development of peace
and the promotion of God's justice.

For in the work of peacemaking, of justice and of
        development,
we see the face of God.

Do you believe in the Son of Man?

(John 9:35)

All of us face questions sometimes,
of what we really believe about God.

To a man just cured of his blindness
Jesus asks the question
of what he believes about him.

A question that brings us up sharply
in the middle of all religious questions.
Questions about church ritual and law
all centre on what we believe of Jesus.

A good and just man, like a historical figure
to be imitated and admired?
Son of God, word of God,
son of Mary and word made flesh?
The one who saves us now
through death and resurrection?

Our beliefs and convictions about human life
follow what we believe about Jesus:

we believe that we are all brothers and sisters,
that we are to care for the world, not dominate it,
that love conquers violence,
and death leads to resurrection.

We relate to God, each other and the world,
more by what we do for him than say about him,
in our efforts to be doers not speakers of this word.

You are looking at him,
he is speaking to you

(John 9:37)

And it's still the same;
we look at the Son of Man
in the people we like,
the people we dislike,
in the poor we see and ignore,
the poor we talk to and help.

We look at the Son of Man
in the stones and earth of a mountain,
in the clouds shadowing a hill with their light.
We hear the Son of Man
in the words of compassion and care
which are whispers and echoes of God's love.

The Son of man is present all around us,
the presence of God enlightening all life,
the care of God in people's care for the poor
and commitment to the works of justice.

When we look at the creation of God –
at the power of nature,
at the love which lasts between people,
at the insights and understanding of who we are,
at the progress of science and communications –
we look at the Son of Man;
for all things were created in life and beauty
through the word of God.
In all of God's creation,
we see that the word was made flesh
and lives among us.

Has no one condemned you?

A question to a woman caught committing adultery
who felt condemned in the public eye,
particularly by the men who brought her to Jesus.

We can be condemned by a look,
which pierces through our self-esteem
like the knife cutting into soft clay;
by words which cut to the heart
like an implement breaking stones;
by a gesture which dismisses us
like a child's cry ignored.

And we can condemn ourselves;
going over our faults again and again
so that a few faults blot out the rest of life.

We feel shame about just being who we are,
like a child's shame after a temper tantrum,
and shame is like a blind on a window
blocking out the light of love.

Religion can condemn also;
giving a message that what is human,
like sexuality, anger, joy, love,
is dangerous, almost wrong.

Shame and condemnation drain our energy,
and half-kill our hopes,
that, like the woman brought to Jesus,
we can be whole again.

Neither do I condemn you,
go away and don't sin any more.

(John 8:11)

The look of Jesus opens us
to realise that each of us is fundamentally good;
that no single experience defines a person.

The look of Jesus invites us to change, and to grow,
so that we know that all of us are people
with a God-given future of promise,
like a river in spate knows there will be calm again;
with a future that is hopeful,
like the rough sea knows there will be an easy tide;
with a future of joy,
like the tree which knows that spring will return.

Hope in ourselves is the foundation of change;
our commitment not to sin again
is based on the full knowledge and consent
that we are fully accepted and loved by God.
Like a tree grows in good soil,
like the child develops with praise,
we can delight in who we are,
in knowing the love of God.

And our hope is based on the goodness of God,
whose love can be trusted to be there always,
hidden sometimes like the moon behind a cloud,
or seeming fragile like a rainbow:
and the love of God has been likened
to the rainbow in the cloud
and the moon that never fades.

What man among you with a hundred sheep, losing one, would not leave the ninety-nine in the desert and go after the missing one till he found it? (Luke 15:4)

Isn't the answer to this question simply 'nobody'.
Who would risk losing all to save one?
Mostly we want to keep what we have,
and don't risk the loss of a hundred euro
to find one we have lost.

A question that will lead us to wonder
what is the essential of God's love –
to value one person so much
almost at the risk of losing the love of the others?

Will God love only those who love him,
forgive only those who ask?
Is God the God of small concerns,
or the one who is concerned about everything
in the lives of the ones he loves.

Forgiveness for God is like a flag of every colour
flying high and joyfully for all his people;
it's God's nature to forgive
as much as it is the nature of rain to be wet.
This is generosity, openness, offered and asked.

Will we live more simply in the West
that people in the East may simply live?
Can we think of risking all we have
to save the life of another?
Then we know what God is like.

There will be more rejoicing in heaven over one repentant sinner than over ninety-nine who have no need of repentance (Luke 15:7)

There is a special joy in God over someone's return,
like the joy in the family when a son or daughter
returns after years of absence.
Or the joy in a real reconciliation after a quarrel,
or when a conflict in a family is really resolved.
Or when peace is made between conflicting groups,
and a nation lives in harmony.

A joy like that was in the heart of Jesus
when he told stories of forgiveness.

God is at his best, if we can say that of God,
when he is forgiving and being merciful.
We can say he is laughing when he is forgiving.
Maybe we don't always know what this means
because we find it hard to be merciful.

Mercy is as much part of God
as water of a river,
as air of a breeze,
as rain is of a cloud.

Mercy covers over wrongs in the past,
with true and lasting forgiveness,
so that sin can be the step to deeper love.

If we can't believe that God is so merciful,
then we're only human,
for mercy among ourselves and with God
is a gift that comes only from heaven.

If you do not believe me when I speak about things in this world, how will you believe me when I speak of heavenly things? (John 3:12)

In the life of Jesus and his meetings with people
there seems to have been a lot of conversation –
debates about religion, marriage, God and death.
And an encouragement to be open to the Spirit
who moves in our lives like the wind through space.

Our minds can be like closed doors,
or full dams or crowded discs.
Winds of change find little space,
and new ideas and new visions perish.

At all ages we can get stuck
with ways of thinking, ways of feeling,
and patterns of faith and love.

We fear to throw ourselves into the future
and to let go of some of the past.

The encouragement of Jesus is
to widen our life-space:
to be open to the stranger and the foreigner,
to believe that the elderly have wisdom to offer
and the young have new ideas.
To believe that everyone's faith
has something new and real to say about God.

The word of God is always new,
challenging old ways of thinking,
inviting us through our life's experiences
to look on the world afresh.

Yet God so loved the world that he gave his only Son, so that everyone who believes in him may not be lost but have eternal life (John 3:16)

We have themes we talk about a lot –
a favourite sport or pastime,
a memorable time of our lives,
hang-ups, prejudices and favourite theories;
what we reminisce about
and what we tell jokes about.

A favourite topic of Jesus was about his Father,
And what he knew of his Father
from his life before he came to earth.

If we know a person,
we have an idea of what's central to their lives.

Jesus learned at the centre of his life –
God delights in what he has made,
in his world and his people,
like parents looking on a newborn baby,
like artists pleased with a painting or sculpture,
like students proud of something learned.

In giving his son,
God has given us a new, saving breath of life,
which unlocks us from the prison
of guilt, self-hatred, greed,
and all that blocks love from surrounding us,

for he loved the world so much
that he gave his Son.

What shall I say:
'Father, save me from this hour'?

(John 12:27)

So much we want to be saved from –
hours of darkness when we lose someone dear,
hours of fear when we think of future old age,
hours of dread about death.

We want to be saved from 'hours',
when we might lose a job,
when we might lose a spouse,
when we might lose a child,
or lose faith and hope in God.

Jesus himself was faced with an hour of fear
that went over many days.
He knew an hour would come when he would
face the darkness of death and of pain,
and he would almost feel he was losing
what was most personal at the centre of his life.

God could not save him from the violence of
        enemies,
nor can God save us from the human losses in life,
nor from the hour of our death.

But he does save us from meaninglessness,
from hopelessness and from despair,
from isolation and from the sense
that nobody cares.

With God it can be like we are in a dark room,
but even though we cannot find the light
we have light enough that God is with us.

But it was for this very reason that I came to this hour

(John 12:28)

We may often wonder why life proves difficult
or why we face trials and pain.
Jesus wondered the same
in days in the desert when he was tempted to run
    away,
or hours in the garden when he felt severe
    loneliness.

Somewhere he found glimpses of meaning,
and he knew that in going through his suffering,
he would prove his love to the end,
and in this love God would be glorified.

Suffering of itself does not glorify or please God,
and sometimes we feel we're like a river
trying to get back up a waterfall.

It is not God's will that we suffer,
through violence or neglect of others,
or through their greed and injustice.

The reason why Jesus came to his hour
was to love God and to love us,
to the edge of the cross
and to the joy of resurrection.

God is glorified in our struggle over hurt and pain,
and what is given in love to God and others
is the reason for coming to any hour of our lives.
And as for Jesus it can be the hour of our freedom.

My God, my God,
why have you forsaken me?

(Matthew 27:46)

Words from the cross, from the death-bed,
a question like an empty echo of former trust,
the feeling of isolation, frustration,
going back with hope to childhood prayers.

Not just the question of a man near death,
but one abandoned and left to fend for himself,
like the child abandoned on the station platform,
the husband at his wife's funeral,
the fear of being alone at the hour of death.

This man, Jesus, whose home was in God,
shares now in human abandonment.

Words sound like an empty foghorn,
pain is the constant companion,
and most friends have fled.

But the mere fact of calling on God,
even in abandonment and rejection,
is finding God.
In the searching is the finding,
in the honest doubt is the root of faith,
and nothing human is foreign to God.

In the cry to God in human anguish,
we meet the cry for companionship from God,
for in our suffering God suffers,
and in God's presence there is rising to new life.

Crying out in a loud voice,
he yielded up his spirit

(Matthew 27:50)

No more words, nothing more to say.
The response to being abandoned
was to shout, cry and
to surrender to what had to be.

Life can take over,
and we flow with it.
In illness, we await healing,
in rejection, we await love again,
in death, we await new life.

Like the chrysalis opening for the butterfly,
like the fruit blossoming on a tree,
like the desert waiting for living streams,
we yield to laws of nature and of life.

There are times when words are empty,
when we sigh or cry,
alone or together.
Like parents with a sick child,
like friends sharing a time of loss,
like people together at a time of violence,
all we can do is share our presence.

Maybe Jesus was glad that a few heard:
the women and one of his apostles,
near enough to share the suffering.

The cry was heard,
and the spirit was reborn.

Have I not told you that if you believe you will see the glory of God?

(John 11:40)

A question to friends of Jesus
who have just suffered the death of their brother:
a question, and like with all Jesus' questions,
a call to faith.

Faith opens the door to new visions
of life and death,
of friendship and intimacy,
of who we were, are and who we can be.
It's more like a verb than a noun, something active:
offering a blessing in every experience of life.

Faith in God and faith in self intertwine;
we trust God not more nor less than
we trust the people closest to us.

In faith we believe that
the glory of God is ourselves fully alive
here and now in all of life.

Alive to the glory of God in others,
of different race, colour, nationality,
so that the foreigner is a welcomed family member,
and everyone is known as a child of God.

Alive to the glory of God in body, mind and soul.
Alive to the joy of a healthy body,
to the freedom of an active mind,
to the wholeness of a full personality.
Alive to the God who lives within us.

Unbind him, let him go free

Inert and frozen in death,
Lazarus is invited to go free
into health and vitality of life.

The story is more than about death,
but about ways in which we get stuck and frozen:
in hopelessness about the future,
in grudges and hurts from the past,
and fears of change in the present.

People bind us and we bind ourselves,
like a river bursting to get free of its dam,
like a flower pushing from a rock into the light,
or a broken down car or stuck foghorn.

True faith cares for self, others and God.
True faith believes in the possibility
of a better future for self and society.
True faith unbinds us from false notions of God
to the truth of what he says about himself,
from selfish concerns to love of others,
from false self-esteem to real self-love.

Community unbinds,
as does prayer, care for the poor
and compassion among us.
Three images of the one God:
the Father to whom we pray,
the Son who loves the poor,
the Spirit of gentle compassion.

Why are you so agitated, and why are these doubts arising in your hearts?

(Luke 24:38)

A question asked of the followers
after they had seen him dead
or heard of his death,
and heard rumours that he was raised from death.

And when they saw him,
present in a new way among them,
who would not be agitated or doubtful?

Death involves us in the world of mystery,
of wondering what happens next,
of wondering what our lives will look like,
or wondering where our loved ones are now.
Most of us can remember the first time
when we first watched a funeral
or touched someone who had died,
and got a sense of something very final.

Commitment involves us in the world of mystery,
and the disciples were confused now
about the big promises they had made,
and the hopes they had in following him.

The mysteries of life, death and choice
bring us close to the presence of God,
and challenge us as to where we put our trust
in these depth moments of life.

In God or self?
In only the seen, or also the unseen?

Everything written about me
has to be fulfilled

(Luke 24:44)

So often we easily think we know who Jesus is;
the disciples had planned his life,
hoping that he would lead them to freedom,
but had not included in their plans
death and rising from death.

There are answers and meanings to life
that are found only in our relationship with God.
In the human heart are two empty caverns or caves:
one to be filled with human friendship,
and one to be opened to God.
Neither will fulfil the other,
as air will not fill the ocean with water
nor will water fill the air with oxygen.

We do not just grow into God:
we allow God grow in us.
We don't just find God by our efforts,
but open our hearts and minds
to be found by God.

With the touch of others in love and friendship,
the touch of God in prayer and ritual,
and the word of God shared in community,
we find that space for God filled in our lives.

We know that answers to the questions of life
are gradually revealed to the open person
in creation, God's word and love among us,
and in his death and rising from death.

What if you saw the Son of Man ascend to where he was before?

(John 6:62)

Many questions begin with 'what if...?'
'What if we really talked to each other...
What if we had forgiven each other...
What if we had spoken before he died...?'
We know things could have been so different.

And this question is something like –
What if we knew who Jesus really is?
What if we knew Jesus from the inside?
What if we fully grasped the mystery of Jesus?

The question came from Jesus
after people complained about him,
that he could give himself as food and drink,
that he was really as generous as he said.

It is a blessing to know someone really well,
to appreciate people for what they are really like,
to understand what someone feels inside.
When we know people's history, we understand
        them,
when we understand, we can forgive,
and when we forgive and understand,
we are on the path to real love.

To know Jesus as he really is,
to know where he came from,
is part of our prayer-quest,
a knowledge that opens to fuller love.

It is the Spirit gives life

Being selective is a human trait:
selecting what we accept in a friend,
selective about a spouse's qualities,
selective about what we share of ourselves,
and all this may be through fear.

The same with Jesus:
we can select what we like or dislike about him.
Some find him too compassionate, not strong,
others see only the demanding side of him.
Or we give him a name,
which we think will sum him up,
so that we think of him as Teacher but not as
        Friend.

The invitation from Jesus is
to look him in the eye, listen to his word,
contemplate what he does,
hear what he says about himself,
all the time going deeper into who he is.

Just as with those we love or with friends,
we know we can never sum them up,
never put a full stop to a page about them,
never the final tone to the notes of a song,
nor the last shade to the colour of a painting.

And if we're open to new visions of Jesus,
we're open to new visions of people,
and this is the gift of the Spirit of Jesus.

39

What matters do you discuss
as you walk along?

(Luke 24:17)

We can imagine their shattered hopes,
two disappointed followers of Jesus.

Dreams of a new and free world seem lost,
and they are going over it again and again,
as we do in telling the story of any loss.
We need to tell how a friend died,
how the house was robbed and valuables taken,
how love got lost along the way in a marriage,
how life disappointed us at times.

The end of Jesus' life on earth
had become for them the whole story
summed up in words, 'We had been hoping'.
Hearts shattered as they thought
that the one who promised life forever was gone.
And they forgot that Jesus spoke of
rising from death and victory and life forever.

They were like a dried up river,
or a computer whose works are stuck,
or a mountain collapsing in a landslide.

Jesus' approach is just to ask 'How are you?'
'What are you talking about?'
The listener from the far side of pain,
who will never forget suffering,
just lets them talk before telling them about himself.
The questions ringing deep in the heart as always.

He explained to them the parts of the scriptures that were about himself

(Luke 24:27)

No condemnation for lack of faith,
no putting them down,
no mention even of betrayal and denial.

Just three people warmly talking and listening
To the real concerns of each other.

A way of finding hope and clarity in bad times
is to talk and be heard,
and then good memories of the past come back,
and hopes for the future can be born.

If we can look at the life of Jesus,
and hear what he says of himself,
our hopes return.
Like the freedom of the flowing river,
the unblocked disc,
the landslide road rebuilt.
Like when we are lifted by an honest conversation
with a friend in a time of trouble.

We hear him saying
that he is friend forever,
that he is resurrection and life.

We can move again,
when we hear the story
of a man's victory over hopelessness and death,
and we know that not only Jesus
but we too are raised from death.

WHO DOES
HE SAY THAT WE ARE?

Do you understand
what I have done to you?

(John 13:12)

A gesture not expected from
the Teacher, the Master, the Lord,
and there was confusion as to why
he humbly washed their feet.

Many times this had happened –
going to dinner with sinners,
welcoming the prodigal son home,
staying with a sinner rather than a pious priest,
curing some and not others.
Jesus was an unpredictable type of person.

Maybe because what he wanted to say
was not always obvious,
especially to the religious people:

that God loves everyone,
that love is more important than law,
that law is to serve love,
and that love of God and neighbour are
one and the same love.

So the unexpected would happen with Jesus:
feet not hands would be washed,
notorious people would come to dinner,
sinners would be publicly forgiven and hugged,
and one day sometime soon after this,
he would walk the earth, raised from death.

I have given you an example so that you may copy what I have done to you

(John 13:15)

The washing of the feet had a purpose after all,
more than cleanliness and good manners.
It was a living witness from Jesus
showing us how to live as his brothers and sisters.

Being disciples means shedding competitiveness,
like taking off shoes for the washing of feet.
There's an equality when we have no shoes on;
being disciples means taking the lowest place,
and being prepared to do the same as Jesus.

So it will mean being like the good Samaritan
or speaking out on the side of the poor;
being committed to life in all its stages,
and caring for the creation of God.

When we ask our questions of him,
Jesus offers meaning and understanding.

Like Peter we will stand again,
our feet washed, our minds instructed,
and our souls made free.

And the way to fulfilment and joy
is in finding the way of God in Jesus,
and living out of his words and example,
recreating, each in our own personality,
the word of God made flesh.

What do you want me to do for you?

(Luke 18:41)

A strange question when a man was blind –
was it not obvious that he would want his sight?
But Jesus seemed to want a person
to get in touch with desires;
the cure was not just automatic.

He asks us what he asked the blind man,
and we may wonder for a while
before we know how to answer.

A generous question
but one that sometimes threatens us.
The heart of God is an outgoing heart,
reaching out to each of us in concern and care,
offering us a meaning and fullness
in our deepest desires and questions.

Often we seem to ask for something good
and it's not given,
like freedom from illness to look after children,
like control over addictions which wreck a family,
like the capacity to control anger and vengeance –
all these seem good, but are not always given.
Can we be open to receiving something better?

We come back to the type of person Jesus is –
wanting to give what is good.
We need time to find out what we really want,
for we are people of many desires.

Receive your sight,
your faith has saved you

(Luke 18:42)

There's a pause between the question and cure,
maybe to test the man's faith,
or to allow the onlookers and ourselves
discover their deepest desires and faith.

Faith itself is a gift.
It saves us

from a meaningless life,
for faith makes sense of all of life;
from the shadows of isolation,
for faith is communal;
from the darkness of hopelessness,
for faith enlightens questions of hope in this age
and of hope for eternity.

In the mystery of our faith we are saved
from many of life's tragedies,
and welcomed into a life
of intimacy with God,
of communion with God's people,
and of doing justice in the world.

And even if the blind man hadn't been cured,
his faith would have saved him
so that he would have been well even while blind.
What he was given was more than his sight.
Like music transforming a human word,
his total faith in God was freshened and deepened.

Can one blind person guide another?

(Luke 6:39)

At any time of life we can be grateful for
the people who guided us well.

Parents, teachers, the people next door,
religious guides, career guides,
pre-marriage directors, counsellors,
the people who influenced by example,
through advice, or by sharing their experience
in times of illness and bereavement,
or who shared encouragement in times of failure,
in times of confusion about bringing up children,
in personal problems like alcoholism and addiction;
another's listening ear and advice was a guide.

We learn in community.
We're more like peninsulas than islands,
more like tributaries than a lone river.
If we miss guidance at key times of life
we may make decisions we later regret,
or feel isolated from others,
and surrounded only by self.

The guidance of friends and others
was the guidance of God:
the hand of God guiding,
the ear of God listening,
the word of God speaking,
the compassion of God touching,
God in the guides of my life.

The fully trained disciple
will always be like the teacher

(Luke 6:40)

The challenge of Jesus
is to be guides, teachers, helpers,
pathfinders for each other,
sharing vision, search and hope.

The journey of life throws up many times
when we need guides,
and when each of us will be a guide.
Without faith, generosity and hope
we can be blind guides to each other.

Good guides see wise ways and point them out,
and have found the true way of life themselves,
living not just on the way but living the way.

Isolation and loneliness can be a feature
of the busy and wealth-seeking world,
and many people are forced to go it alone.

We need the shared companionship of
being guides to each other
in the way of humanity, parenting, faith,
in ways of prayer and love,
and of getting through dark times;
at times like this we want to be able to
enter the world of the other,
and be good guides on the way to fuller life.
People of vision and of hope,
excited by Jesus' vision of life,
leading others in the way of God.

Can you not buy two sparrows for a penny?

(Matthew 10:29)

People would think little of sparrows –
they seem worth nothing.

Cheap to buy,
even beautiful for a while,
but easily disposed of.

We have various ways of valuing people and things:
the resources of the earth may be used
to benefit a nation and everyone,
or just the few, as when we destroy a forest
to ensure a ready supply of paper.

The air is polluted, and we may ignore
issues of health
and the welfare of the next generation.

Even human life can seem expendable –
protection or destruction of life before birth,
ignoring of the elderly and their needs,
valuing people for what they have
and dismissing them if they are poor.

The two sparrows seemed of no use,
and much of creation is viewed like that.

The question of Jesus is a simple question from
the One in whom all things were made,
and whose love and enjoyment of creation
seemed to extend from the smallest leaf
to the beauty of each human person.

No need to be afraid;
you are worth more than many sparrows
(Matthew 10:31)

Like the river waters at the same time
the flourishing cash-promising crop
and the seemingly useless flower;
like the sun shines on everyone,
rich and poor, even the criminal,
so the eye of God
looks with care and love on all.

We can be scared by that all-seeing eye of God,
particularly if we feel it sees us
at our weakest, unguarded and mean moments.
It may seem the sort of eye that catches us out.

The eye of God is the eye that looks with love,
like the friend's eye looks on us with affirmation,
and with joy and humour.
When we are looked on by God,
it is the look that valued the sparrow,
which was noticed and loved in its fall to the
        ground.

And in the eye of God we see the life of heaven,
a love that is always there for us,
as reliable as the sunset and sunrise of every day;
a forgiveness that covers over our guilt and shame,
as consistent as the evergreen pine tree,
and an invitation to enjoy that love
as life-giving as the ocean
that breaks each day on the shore.

Why do you observe the splinter in another's eye and never notice the plank in your own?
(Luke 6:41)

Aren't we all a mixture of virtues and faults,
good points and bad points?
Indeed often what we dislike in another
is what we dislike in ourselves.

We may live with a mixture
of condemnations and judgements about others,
excusing them one moment
and condemning them the next,
changeable like the weather.

The speck of dust in another's eye
that is driving us mad
has been formed through life's experiences.
We all have a story of life
which partly explains the way
we behave.
Rejection in the past may make us fearful,
abuse may make us isolated,
marked as we are by life's experiences,
as storms shape stones,
and floods cause landslides,
and things look different forever.

Jesus knew that,
and he knew also
that we miss faults and failings in ourselves
but see them in others.

Take the plank out of your own eye first, and then you will see clearly enough to take out the splinter in another's eye (Luke 6:42)

The invitation is to look at ourselves,
how we may present ourselves to others.
We may look out at the speck of dust
through a beam of wood in our own eye.
Not with condemnation nor harshness
but in the reality of the mixture
of the good and bad in us all.

The eye of Jesus looks at each of us
with wonder and delight in our goodness,
with healing and forgiveness for our faults.

And when we admit that it is only a speck of dust
in the eye of another, and not a total fault,
then we may notice that the beam in our own eye
is in fact a speck of dust:
a fault we over-emphasise
or our expectation of perfection.

Can we look at ourselves wholly,
seeing the best in ourselves and the worst,
as a snowflake is both harsh in its coldness
and beautiful in the light reflected in its colour;

can we view ourselves with the wisdom of God,
less harsh in judgements of self
and then more understanding and loving to others,
letting out the warmth of God's love?

Love touches our harshness with gentleness.

If the smallest things therefore are outside your control, why worry about the rest?

(Luke 12:26)

Many important things are outside our control:
our name, nationality, our religion,
the colour and look of our body,
the sharpness and brightness of our mind,
the openness and capacity of our spirit –
all has been given.

We do not know when we shall die,
nor what sort of old age, if any, we shall have.

In small and large areas of life,
much is not chosen, but accepted.

To worry about the future is only human,
but it saps the energy.
Jesus' advice is to be concerned,
but not to worry.

All of us have worried about things
that in fact never happened,
about people who could look after themselves well;
and worry only destroys our peace.

So much beauty and goodness was never planned:
flowers, scenery, birds of the air,
and the way a baby cries or laughs.

We are blessed if we put worry and anxiety
with God who knows what we need.

Your Father knows well you need them

(Luke 12:30)

A loving hand guides our lives,
a loving force guides our world,
a loving and personal God is involved
in the past, present and future of our lives.

God knows each of us by name,
by the history of our lives, by our hopes.
Our peace and freedom from worry,
comes partly from the love God has for each.
And then we have more space to solve problems.

A love which touches us
when we are worried, anxious, fearful.
Like the sparkle in the middle of a diamond,
like the colour in the middle of a thread,
like the rain in the middle of a cloud.

Always there, essential
to the diamond, thread or cloud,
but not itself the diamond, cloud or thread.

Being involved in the love of God
brings the deepest happiness –
could the desert be happy without sand
or the sun happy without light?

All else will then be viewed in this light.
Our anxiety about past, present or future
is lived within the environment
of the love of God.

If you love those who love you what thanks can you expect?

(Luke 6:32)

It's only human to love those who love us,
to give gifts in return for gifts,
kindness in return for kindness,
and to treat others as they treat us.

Something in us wants to be thanked
when we put ourselves out for someone,
to be praised for what we do for others.

We need this sort of affirmation,
this sort of praise and thanks,
like the flower needs light to grow,
like the tree needs water to flourish,
like a light needs current to shine.

Even Jesus himself wanted to be thanked.

But it doesn't satisfy fully.
We know there is a sense of fulfilment
when we do something for no reward –
when we love a son or daughter in bad times
just because she is a son or daughter.
The greatest love is unselfish
and we see it in the love of parents for children,
and the love of children for ageing parents.

Our thanks is like a key to joy in who we are
and to a deepening friendship with God.

Instead, love your enemies and do good.
Then you will have a great reward

There is another type of love,
more rare than the love that looks for no return:
the love for someone who did us wrong.
There seems to be praise for a love
which has no sense outside its own motivation.

It is like the forgiving love of Jesus
who loved till the end of the cross.
Never a human achievement
but a divine gift,
prayed for, hoped for,
encouraged by others' forgiving,
not easily understood.
The urge for vengeance is a strong motivation
tempered only by the gift of God's forgiveness.

'No fool like an old fool,'
they said of the father of the prodigal son,
who welcomed home the son who had ruined him.

Forgiveness of enemies sometimes converts them,
and it converts those who witness it.
Tolerance of enemies and understanding of them
is a strong link in the ladder of heaven and earth,
a way we are most like God.
And a sure sign of the presence of God among us,
like a tree flowering in a ruined building site,
or a wind blowing cool in the heat wave.
Always the reminder of God's new life.

Why do you call me, 'Lord, Lord' and not do what I say?

(Luke 6:46)

Words can be easy –
promises can be lightly made,
and with difficulty followed through.
Prayers can be said, with little real prayer,
words can be spoken with little love.

Love is proved in what we do rather than in words.
Religious words can be empty or full.
For words to be sincere, we look for the action.
For prayer to be genuine, we look for the fruits.
For love to be genuine, we look for commitment.

It can even be easy to mouth the word of God
and the words flit away on the wind,
or like bubbles disappear into thin air.

Words can encourage and build up,
like scaffolding which supports a building.
Words can be false and diminish us,
like polluted air suffocating us,

We can pray 'Lord, Lord' and be meaning 'me, me',

Calling him Lord is easy,
working for the Lordship of God,
the coming of truth, compassion and love,
bringing glory to God and peace among people,
is a lifetime's living out of all we say and promise.

Everyone who comes to me and listens to my words and acts on them is like a man who has built his house on rock (Luke 6:47)

Faith grows in action.
Living out the gospel will strengthen our faith,
like living out love strengthens a marriage;
living out the implications of any commitment
strengthens that commitment.

We look for a rock in our lives,
something that is consistent,
we look also for a foundation in our lives
that cannot be taken away,
and for a flow in our lives
that unites choices and feelings.

We look for and desire
a flow in the source of our activity,
a rock in the motivation of our lives,
a foundation for the reasons for our love.

Living out the word of God
is a way of entering more deeply
into the word of God
and the life of God,
and of finding rock not sand
at the basis of our lives.

We learn to love in the ways we love others.
We learn to love God in the ways
we try to pray sincerely
and to live out what God asks of us.

What gain then is it to have won the whole world and so to have lost or ruined one's very self? (Luke 9:25)

We can get success in business or civic life
and lose honesty and compassion;
we can get influence and power in our jobs
and lose tolerance and understanding;
we can get knowledge in looking for happiness
and lose generosity and peace;
we can list achievements in many areas
of church, family, state and job,
and not know who we are.

We are not the sum of our achievements,
and our reality is more than can be seen.

As the depths of the sea
give home to rocks, fish and colour,
our body gives home
to deeper layers of personality
that are larger than anything we do.
Our mind gives home to a variety
of ideas and insights
that are never exhausted.

We can become a product of ads and of pressures,
winning what looks good,
and losing what lasts for good.
In trying to enjoy all around us,
we fail to enjoy what's inside us:

the love we share and the good we do,
and just who we are ourselves,
each of us the delight of God.

Those who are ashamed of me and of my words, the Son of Man will be ashamed of them when he comes in glory (Luke 9:26)

Choosing the way of life and of God
may create opposition,
and we know the feelings of being out of step with
        others
when we choose what goes against the normal.

Personality can grow or be diminished,
like any tree, plant or flower of creation.
What we are called to be in our future
may be stunted by other voices
that point us away from goodness,
and we settle for something less good.

When we turn our back on goodness,
we turn away from God;
and when we turn from following
what we know is true and right,
we are like signposts pointing the wrong way;
trying to find lasting happiness and wholeness
in places that promise happiness only for a while.

We look for living water
where the springs have been muddied
with false directions
on the road of loving and being loved.

Can we allow ourselves realise
that when we are ashamed
of our commitment to be good,
that God is also lessened in us?
For we and God are one.

Who touched me?

(Mark 5:31)

Another strange question in a crowd;
many must have jostled and pushed him,
like a crowd trying to shake hands with a celebrity;
or wanting to be healed,
like a crowd trying to touch a holy person.

There is a need for healing in us all –
trying to move on from wounds of hurt and grief,
letting go of bitterness and grudges,
to live more freely and happily.
The woman's illness was physical and also spiritual.
She wanted to think well of herself again
and not have to hide her face with shame in public.

We carry the scars of what people said about us,
scars of rejection, abuse and dismissal
and of being treated unjustly.
We carry them like a rock carries the marks of a
        chisel,
or the mountain side carries the ruin of a landslide,
and a tree the marks of age in its wood.

We laugh through tears of rejection
and cry with memories of abuse or neglect,
hope that we can walk and run freely again,
that we can trust others and enjoy friendship again.

And we want to meet someone who touches
with the touch of care, compassion and love.
The touch of faith called out the healing power
of the love and compassion of God in Jesus.

Your faith has restored you to health;
go in peace and be free of your complaint
(Mark 5:34)

There are times in life when we know we need
something more than helping words.
We find ourselves drawn to a solution to problems
or to a wholeness and integrity of life.

Like when we get the second wind
on the final climb to a summit of a mountain;
or find the space and loving energy
to spend time with someone who is ill;
or when we forgive and accept back once again
the child who is struggling with addictions.

Somehow we find faith in ourselves and in others,
and we live in a deeper peace.

Or when we come to moments of silence and prayer
and just allow ourselves be present to God,
not pretending to be any better than we are,
but knowing our time with God is a time of faith.

There's a healing then and a wholeness
like when water gushes on its way through rocks,
or a flower pushes its way through an opening in
        stone.

Faith is something alive in our personality
and we know it touches something in Jesus:
the gift of our faith is touched again
and faith becomes a strong foundation
of peace of mind, body and spirit.

Do you want to be well again?

(John 5:7)

At the pool in the middle of the city they waited
to get to the water first when it moved.
With the man of the thirty-eight year wait
Jesus checked out did he want to get well.

Jesus never cures without some request:
he wants to know do we want to be healed.
Do we want to be freed of the anger we carry,
or of the guilt that keeps us down,
or the grudge we nurture till it festers?
Or can we let those who have died
really go to God,
and while we miss them
we can move on ourselves?

Sometimes we find it hard to let go
of bitterness, anger, grief, sadness.
Like old furniture crowding a room
though it all seems part of the house.

What keeps us from deeper freedom
can be like a flag we fly unknown to ourselves;
or like an ugly piece of art
which we would like to throw out
but then the space would be empty.
All of us carry burdens and wounds from our past,
as the man at the pool had been ill so long.

Can we really say to the Lord,
Yes, I want to be well, I want to be healed?

Get up, pick up your sleeping mat, and walk

(John 5:9)

A good chat with a friend over a recent loss
and we can feel a relief and a freedom
that is a gift of God and of a friend.

A conversation with a counsellor and we feel
we are letting go past experiences that
seem still to hurt and be as recent as last night's
      dream.

A time of sincere prayer with God
and we know we can look on hurt
with a wider vision;
and the remarks that wounded
no longer take centre stage
or speak so loudly in the memory.

We know what it is like
to pick up the burdens of our emotions,
like a person lies on a stretcher,
and walk free of feelings and moods that
have hindered love and joy in life.

We walk free in the help of others
with whom we can share our life;
with whom our secrets are safe
and the grubby side of life is accepted.

And we know each of us can do that for another,
so that a friend, a child, a spouse, another,
can live more freely in friendship and faith.

Were not all ten made clean?
The other nine, where are they?

(Luke 17:17)

Only one man came back to thank God
for the cure Jesus had done.
He was a foreigner, an outsider, not 'one of us',
and in the eyes of many, a reject.

There's an expectation in Jesus;
he hopes that we would praise God
for what God does for us.

To be grateful for
the beauty of a mountain and a sea,
the sensitivity of a friend in trouble,
the commitment of someone to the poor,
the life of prayer and worship,
the many talents and gifts of self and others,

for the work for justice and peace,
for the welcome given to a refugee,
for the aid given to a developing country,
for the time given to the elderly and sick –
can be a daily prayer.

Gratitude brings us in touch with our true humanity;
it's like the roots of a tree deep in the earth,
like the flow of a water in a stream:
neither stream nor tree could be themselves
without water nor roots.

And when we see gratitude in the poorest child,
we know we have met something very human,
and have met God made flesh in his people.

Stand up and go on your way,
your faith has saved you

Faith grows with gratitude,
like seeds flourish in the heat of the sun,
or friendship with shared secrets.

The true follower of Jesus
lives in the atmosphere of thanks.
Even the illnesses of life –
bereavements, disappointments,
all we call the cross of life –
can bring us into depths of ourselves,
or into the compassion and care of others,
and there are times we can be grateful for the cross.

Nothing in life cannot be a blessing
that brings us nearer to God.

Faith is made strong by many people –
parents, teachers, friends, ministers,
by experiences of life which bring depth to faith,
and in this thanking story of Jesus,
faith is made strong by a person
other religious people looked down on.

God, as close to us as the air we breathe,
as close to us as the light to the colour,
can speak to us and touch us through everyone,
even a person who seems far from God.

Nobody is far from God
for God lives within each of us.

Who is my mother,
who are my brothers?

(Matthew 12:48)

Should there not be an obvious answer:
or was there a trick in it?

Among people for whom no relationship
was more important than family,
the question might tempt Jesus
away from his work and back to his family.
Pressure on Jesus to become just like so many
        others,
and live to please his family only,
for did they not think he was mad?

Family can be a negative pressure:
do I care for family only?
Do I spend myself so much for family
that I have time for nothing else?
Do I waver from truth
to stay united with the family?

We are related to each other like vine to branches,
we draw physical life from our family,
all who are created in the image of God
share the life of the spirit.

With Jesus we discover that family is wider than
blood brothers and sisters,
and that people give up even family,
and the joy and grace of wife, husband, son or
        daughter
for love of the larger family of God.

Whoever does the will of my Father
is my mother, sister and brother
(Matthew 13:50)

We are part of the family of humanity and of faith.
Jesus takes the closest of human relationships
and without devaluing them
broadens them to include everyone.

All who try to live in the spirit of God
live in the home of God;

whether poor or rich,
our own nationality or another,
immigrants and emigrants,
old and young,
those we like and those we dislike:
these are brothers and sisters of Jesus.

When we look at mother or father,
we see the ones who gave us birth;
they are also our brothers and sisters in God.
Friends become more than friends,
but are family members in Jesus Christ.
All who are called outsiders
are insiders in the family of God.
Each of us carries the fragrance of God.

When we gather in the presence
of the mystery of God,
we gather in a new relationship
to the whole human race,
adopted children of God,
and brothers and sisters of each other.

Why are you asleep?
Had you not the strength to watch one hour?
(Mark 14:37)

Maybe his need for companionship
made him ask the question.
A desire to teach the disciples by the example
of how he would face the coming hour.

No condemnation –
he makes an excuse or explanation for them:
their strength had gone.

Can we look around us and waken up
to the million children who die monthly of hunger?
The millions also who are not educated?
The women subjected to violence?
The slavery still a way of life for thousands?
The poverty and need under our own eyes?
We sleep today at the passion of God's people.

Can we be aware of the pain of friends and
colleagues
when we find out that they went through bad times
and nobody seemed to hear or care?

In the desert of suffering,
the storms of pain,
the coldness of grief,
we can be streams bringing new growth,
hands and hearts that warm cold times,
and the calm which eases the suffering of others.

Then we are awake to the suffering of God
in his many bodies of pain in his people today.

You should be awake and praying not to be put to the test. The spirit is willing but the flesh is weak (Mark 14:38)

Often we say that we hope
we don't have to go through big trials –
that a child will never be seriously ill,
that marriage will not grow cold and die,
that commitments will not become empty,
that jobs will not be lost,
that faith will not diminish or fade.

We know the weakness of the human spirit,
as we marvel at its strength.
We want to be strengthened in our soul,
so that we can walk strong in life,
and offer the same strength to others.

Jesus speaks from experience
and knew the ups and downs of spirit
in the hours of struggle in the desert.
He knew that the love of the Father
would in fact sustain him, and keep him safe,
even though he wanted the comfort of the disciples.

If we are awake to all that happens in life,
alert to pain and to struggle,
we can open the door to the strength of God.

Sharing life with God means sharing fears and pain,
and finding new strength in our friendship with him.

Woman, why turn to me?

(John 2:4)

A question asked to get a couple out of a fix,
and it seems that Jesus doesn't care.

Does he care
that health is breaking up,
that a child is so ill,
that a parent's death is so painful,
that the family has no employment,
that millions starve,
that millions are homeless,
that terrorism seems victorious.
We can list the litany of questions
to a God who says that he cares,
and we wonder when his hour will come.

We yearn for the care of God
and long to know that he is close.

Do we care...
that millions starve
and millions are homeless?
That a friend is suicidal,
and another is battling with family addiction?
When will be their hour?

Care is something we long for:
to care for others and to be cared for.
When people care,
then the hour of God's care has come.

Fill the jars with water

The action of Jesus at this wedding
is the care of God for all of us.
Something new happens in our lives
when we allow ourselves live the way of God.
and God's hour is our hour.

Living in love is living in the way of God,
like the air we breathe,
like the wind on our face;

like air that sometimes consoles us
or other times almost chokes us,
as God and life draws us into the pain of others;
or the wind on our faces can be calm or stormy,
as God is found within storms of confusion and
          doubt,
as well as in the calm and hope of easier times.

To do what he says –
his advice to the waiters when the wine was gone,
and it seemed ridiculous to fill jars with water.

At times the way of Jesus seems mad –
it is the way of compassion for everyone,
of welcome to the stranger,
of forgiveness to the violent,
of any way of sure and certain hope
in the influence and the victory of good.

In the fullness of care and help among people
is the glory of God made visible.

Where is your faith?

(Luke 8:25)

A question asked in the middle of a storm at sea;
one often asked in the middle of life's storms.

Throughout life, faith develops and grows,
through its moods and times of doubt and
            confusion,
like the weather on the lake,
like the ups and downs of love;

we wonder and we ask ourselves
where our faith is
when we feel cold towards God
and cold towards people.

He rebuked the storm
and questioned the disciples,
rather than questioning the storm
and rebuking the disciples –
expecting that faith
has its times of doubt and certainty,
and that there is faith
in times when feelings of trust are low.

Faith is like many things –
like an umbrella sheltering from rain and sun,
like stepping stones hidden in a river,
like a lighthouse in the fog,
guiding, challenging, sustaining us
in the changes of belief and unbelief.

He gives orders even to winds and waves and they obey him

(Luke 8:25)

Sometimes there are signs,
and faith grows.
Other times no signs.

Signs of faith come simply –
the helping hand when times are rough,
the beauty of a flower which lifts the spirit,
the moment of peace in prayer,
the closeness of God in ritual,
the faith shared in community.

We can be amazed sometimes
at the ways we find faith strengthened.
Memories of family faith,
hymns sung that remind us of God,
and images filling the mind,
like our bodies being surrounded by light.

Jesus seems to expect that faith will be always
        there,
questioning yet hopeful,
that there will be times when only faith guides us,
and creates a trust that is strong but seems distant.

Always caring – our God,
even when it seems he sleeps.
Always the call – that we do not sleep
through others' tough moments.
And the openness to welcome and look for faith,
blowing like the wind, gently or loudly,
always a gift gratefully awaited and received.

Does not scripture say, 'My house will be called a house of prayer for all the peoples?'
(Mark 11:17)

It cost a lot to get into the house of God those
            days;
people had to buy their offerings and then enter,
and the offerings were fixed by the priests.
The poor were at the gate or found another place
to enter into the presence of the God of all peoples.

Like the soil receiving clean and dirty water,
like the air receiving moisture and pollution,
like fire accepts all it is given,
the heart of God like the house of God
is open to all,
and the first place of worship is the human heart.

Memories here of churches
that had cheaper and dearer seats
and the poor were marginalised.

There is no back seat in God's house,
no place to hide except in God's heart,
no place to pretend except in our own heart.

Challenging words:
any changes in the house of God
seem to upset religious people.

What is really suspect in the house of God
is when we never change ourselves
or never discover deeper community.

But you have turned it into a robber's den
(Mark 11:18)

On the surface the building was beautiful,
the incense smelled sweet
and the music was praised.

The temple of God was clean and pure,
and the leaders were unfazed
until someone said that things could be different.

That it could be a place for all the people,
that the cost of worship was robbing the poor,
and when they heard that,
they wanted to do away with him.

No place for the foreigner or refugee;
nobody barred them but the place was organised
so that they would not feel welcome.
No place for the ones people looked down on
or people who might be publicised as sinners.
A place at the table of God only for those
who thought and acted (and paid) like 'us'.

The heart of God feels the division of people,
feels the rejection of those whose lives are different
and are diminished in the very place
they might find wholeness and hope.

When we rob people of their dignity
in the name of religion or worship,
we have turned the house of God
into a den of robbers,
and the crucifixion of God begins.

What can we say
the kingdom of God is like?

(Mark 4:30)

We can spend years on favourite questions,
about life and death, love and hope,
about nationalism and freedom.
People often say things like,
'I've spent years wondering about that'.

Or you can live with someone for years
and wonder what makes them tick,
what is essential to them,
and as you know them
you know what is at their centre.

Or you can spend years on a discovery –
creating a new species of flower,
mesmerised by some scientific problem,
even becoming expert in a language.

Jesus' prime concern was to proclaim this kingdom.
He healed the sick, cured some who couldn't walk,
preached the gospel to the poor and downtrodden
to show us what the kingdom of God is like.

Did he not struggle with the question
as people tried to persuade him
it was a political kingdom and he the king?

When he asked what it was like,
he was asking the most serious question
and the question dearest to him.

It's like a mustard seed, which at its time of sowing is the smallest of all the seeds on earth (Mark 4:31)

Is this much of an answer
to one of Jesus' dearest questions?

The best things in life grow and mature slowly –
our best friendships matured over time,
romance may grow from infatuation into love.
Love takes its time to know and value someone.
Freedom in our lives grows slowly.
Any knowledge or insight grows with struggle.

The kingdom of God grows slowly,
like small seeds grow into big trees,
like tiny streams become huge rivers.

It's more like the life's blood within a person,
than a collection of documents and buildings.

The kingdom of God in a person's life
is a shelter for many;
like the mustard seed shelters many as a tree,
and birds find rest there,
and a home not just for themselves
but for their young.

To be in the kingdom is to be a person for others,
So that many can rest and
be refreshed in our shadow of care and love.

Do you believe at last?

(John 16:31)

The journey of faith takes time,
like any big journey in life.
Like love grows between people
on the journey towards marriage,
like our friendships grow in life
faith changes and matures through years.

The disciples took time to get to know Jesus
and to take in what he was trying to teach them.

We sometimes expect faith to be there for us,
to be a ready-made package,
or like having credit we draw on;
it's more a growing relationship through
different experiences of life.

We believe in different ways at different times –
the pain and losses of our lives effect our faith,
bringing us closer to God or we feel distant;
over the years we find the spaces for God in life
and we believe like the friends of Jesus
that he came from God and goes to God.

As we do ourselves.
There are moments when we are caught up
in beauty or love, prayer or understanding;
when we are stripped of human resources and know
there is a peace and a presence surrounding us;
there are times when we are certain in the heart
that God exists, loves and is close to us.

I have told you all this
that you may find peace in me

(John 16:33)

There are many sources of peace in life:
the peace of mind and heart we long for.
Some bring peace for a while,
some bring a lasting peace.

The peace of success which lasts for a while
after something has gone really well
or after victory in sport or study;
the peace of finishing something which took time.
Many are the of sources of peace.

There is peace between people,
when we find happiness in love and friendship,
when a conflict has been resolved,
when we work together for others' good.

We long for peace like the rose wants its colour,
like the bird looks for the wind to support its flight.
We are people made for the peace which lasts
        forever.

This is something of the peace Jesus offers,
the peace of God glimpsed in human peace,
and we know it could last.

The troubles of life and of faith
can lead us into a deeper peace
if we can share these in love
with others and with God.
And faith gives us the peace
we need in life's troubles.

How many loaves have you?

(Mark 6:38)

A scene when people were needy and hungry,
and Jesus wanted to feed them.

Today Jesus would ask:
How much food have you in the world
and millions starve?
How much is spent on arms each year,
while people could be cured of disability?
Is the budget for communications satellites
more than the health care budget?
Are there not more than enough resources
to educate all the children of the world?

And what about irrigation and clean water
instead of research into new fashions?
And what about caring for the sick and dying
when so much is wasted on conferences
where so much is said and so little is done?

Like the apostles we wonder what this would mean
to so many people in need;
we always think we don't have enough.

The world has enough, said Gandhi,
for our need,
but not enough for our greed.

In the hours he spent with the poor and the
     deprived,
Jesus' question challenges our generosity:
'How many loaves have you?'

Then he broke the loaves and handed them to the disciples to distribute among the people (Mark 6:41)

What followed this question is mysterious.
Did the loaves just expand and feed everyone?
Or is the story about the generosity of God
who has made enough for his people;
and the call on all of us is
to share and give of what we have.

We grasp that the will of God
is a world where people have equal rights
to education, medical care,
shelter and religious freedom;
and we know there is enough space
and raw materials in the world
to build a home for every child of God.

And that for each of us there is help
in times of anxiety, confusion and fear,
if only we could open ourselves to others
in trust rather than close up in fear,
nourishing and being nourished in time of need.

We need to feel the urgency of
the question of the apostles –
'How can we feed all these people?'
We need to bring that question to Jesus
And allow our hearts be touched with his care
for the poorest of the poor.
With him we can really desire and work for
a world more equal for the life of all.

Have you caught anything, friends?

(John 21:5)

All of us want to make a difference
in our family, friendships, work
and in what we give our hearts to.
We hope that the world will be
somewhat more loving,
just and a better place
for our passing through.

We want the gospel to come alive in
who we are, in our words and actions.
We want something good to be caught from us,
a desire flowing within us from God.

We want the assurance
that our love is never wasted,
that it will always bear fruit,
like a river waters distant places,
and the mist moistens the earth.

The question after a night's aimless fishing,
asked with friendship and genuine interest.
Something like –
'How have you made a difference for today?'
'How has love been caught through you?'

For where love and compassion,
truth and justice have been caught
one from another in life,
then God has been caught.

Throw your net out to starboard
and you'll find something

(John 21:6)

In working for love, justice, compassion,
we are directing our commitments and hopes
to be like his.

In the confusion of how to love,
he invites us to follow how he loved to the end.
In the confusion of how to find meaning in life,
he invites us to look deep into the questions of life;
he has seen where life abounds fully,
as he could see life in the lake.

Our friendship with God stretches our love
like we stretch the bow to fly the arrow,
and our love goes deeper and grows more joyful
when we're united with his love.

We look back on some times in life
and wonder what we have caught.
We want full hands and a full heart,
with memories of love and goodness
that made a difference to people,
when we find ourselves in the twilight of life.

The question of Jesus
touches that deep hope within us,
to do the best in life;
looking to him and with him
our efforts bear more fruit,
to do the world a world of good.

DONAL NEARY SJ

Do you love me?

(John 21:17)

This question of Jesus to Peter
sums up many of the questions of Jesus.

It was asked of someone –
who seemed an ordinary enough man –
who had struggled with questions
raised by what he saw and heard of Jesus,
who had followed him for years,
and promised to follow him for ever,
but who had denied he ever knew him;
and who had from a distance seen his death.

All through the years of Galilee,
Peter would have pondered over questions,
read the scriptures, resisted their call,
followed the attraction of the call,
talked to others about what Jesus meant
and what religion was about.

He would have pondered over the empty tomb;
knowing that love is born in the death
that was the shadow hour of resurrection.

It's the question that gives depth and meaning,
to every friendship, commitment and marriage –
do you love me?
A human question with an eternal resonance,
for if the answer is yes –
to a person or to God –
it is love that lasts forever.

Feed my sheep

(John 21:17)

Religion can get mixed up;
what is of minor importance can seem so urgent.

Places of worship,
laws about marriage and sexuality,
fasting, almsgiving and prayer,
all can have a rating they don't deserve.

The real challenge of religion
comes in the question about love –
about thinking of another before oneself,
about putting ourselves out for another,
about making another's concerns our own.
It means patience and kindness in the family,
tolerance and understanding with friends,
and willingness to suffer for others,
and to become men and women for others.

The real challenge of religion comes in knowing
that loving God means especially loving people,
when they are weak, poor and seem at their worst.

We look at those the world doesn't like,
whom society ignores or forgets in its planning,
who seem to offer little to the competitive world,
and hear the call of Jesus,
to love him and feed him in these.

And often they are the people who, having little
        else,
feed many with their love.